The Best 50
SCONES

Karen L. Pepkin

NITTY GRITTY COOKBOOKS

Lanham • New York • Boulder • Toronto • Plymouth, UK

NITTY GRITTY COOKBOOKS
4501 Forbes Boulevard, Suite 200, Lanham, Maryland 20706
www.rowman.com
10 Thornbury Road, Plymouth PL6 7PP, United Kingdom
Distributed by National Book Network

ISBN: 978-1-55867-338-0 (pbk.: alk paper)

Cover design: Frank J. Paredes
Cover photography: John A. Benson
Food styling: Randy Mon
Illustration: Nora Wylde

The paper used in this publication meets the minimum requirements of American National Standard for Information Sciences—Permanence of Paper for Printed Library Materials, ANSI/NISO Z39.48-1992. Printed in the United States of America

DEDICATION

Thanks to my colleagues in Special Education Services Dept., Region 4 ESC, Houston, TX. Their valuable feedback enabled me to perfect these recipes. As always, thanks to Wendell C. Taylor, for his love and support.

(A LITTLE) ABOUT SCONES

Although it is generally accepted that scones are British, the word 'scone' may come from the Dutch word, schoonbroot, meaning "fine bread." The scone is also a cousin to the American biscuit.

ORGANIZATION OF THIS BOOK

This book is organized into four parts: *"Scones and Fruit"* (fresh and dried fruits); *"Scones and Goodies"* (including nuts, flavored chips, coconut flakes); *"Not Your Granny's Scones"* (savory scones, containing vegetables, cheeses, herbs); and *"Serving Suggestions"*. Suggestions for glazes are also included in the recipes.

Read these tips before you begin. First make the recipe exactly as written. Afterwards, feel free to be creative and make adaptations. Happy "sconing" and enjoy!!

TIPS FOR SHAPING, BAKING AND SERVING SCONES

- Ovens and climates vary. Always try baking a recipe using the minimum time indicated, and if necessary, increase in increments of 2 to 3 minutes until desired consistency is reached. If scone is too dry, decrease baking time in the same increments.

- Some scones are better warm, especially those with cheese. If they are cool or room temperature, put scones in the microwave for 30 seconds.

- Although you can substitute margarine for butter, it will affect the taste and consistency.

- Heavy cream can be substituted for half-and-half.

- Whether you use a rolling pin or your hands, it is important that the thickness of the dough remain consistent. If not, parts of the scone can be over or under baked.

- As with muffins, cakes, and cookies, there is a lot of creativity and flexibility in baking scones. Juices can be interchanged, various types of chips, nuts, seeds, spices, herbs, and grated cheeses can be substituted or added; the only thing to keep in mind is how they will affect the texture. Review the recipes which are similar to your creation and use them as a guide.

- Fruits have excess moisture and if not removed, scones become gummy or crumbly. Do remove excess moisture when instructed.

- Egg wash can be used to give the scones a shiny finish, and to help other ingredients stick to the surface. Simply brush on egg yolk. Some people prefer a glaze to add sweetness and "dress up" the scones. If this is your preference, see *Serving Suggestions,* page 5, for glaze recipes.

- Sprinkling ingredients on top of the scone (seeds, zest, chopped nuts, etc.), provides a way of identify the different varieties, if you are serving multiple scones.

- Traditional British scones are not sweet. They are served with "clotted cream" and jam. If this is your preference you can reduce the amount of sugar in any of the recipes, but remember this will change the intensity of the flavor.

- In this book I shape scones into triangles, but just as cookies can be shaped in a variety of ways, you can make scones round or square or even into more intricate shapes however, you must use a rolling pin, and constant reworking the dough will affect the texture after it is baked. The next section includes serving suggestions and square and circular shapes are more appropriate for some of these recipes.

- Never store scones warm; they absorb moisture and become crumbly and wet. Scones can be frozen in freezer bags, but not indefinitely. They pick up flavors from the freezer. Limit freezer time to a week. Scones can also be kept in a plastic bag at room temperature or in the refrigerator for 2 to 3 days.

SERVING SUGGESTIONS

SCONE FRENCH TOAST

Mix 1 egg with ½ cup half-and-half. Cut 3 scones in half to make 6 thin slices. Let scones soak in egg mixture for 30 to 45 minutes. Fry in butter, until brown on each side. Serve with maple or other flavored syrups, jam, jelly, fruit toppings, or for something different, mix a tablespoon of Raspberry Chipotle dressing with a cup of seedless raspberry jam. Serve over scone French toast.

EGGS BENEDICT

Make scones round and replace English muffins with scones split in half.

LUNCH SCONES

Using any of the *"Not Your Granny's Scones"*, serve with soup or salad or use as a base for sandwiches, as suggested below.

CHICKEN OR SHRIMP SALAD ALA SCONES

Choose your favorite chicken or shrimp salad recipe and serve over any of the following scones: *Traditional, Honey Wheat, Lemon, Mango Mango, Poppy Seed Onion, Sesame* or *Apricot Peach.*

DINNER SCONES

Use scones as dinner rolls. *Honey Wheat, Jalapeno Corn, Sesame,* and *Onion Poppy Seed* work well.

HOT OPEN-FACED SANDWICHES

Split scones open and ladle gravy over. Pile hot roast beef, turkey or other sliced meats on top and finish with additional gravy. *Honey Wheat, Poppy Seed Onion* and *Jalapeño Corn* work well.

SCONE BREAD PUDDING

Try replacing the bread in your bread pudding with leftover thinly sliced scones. Use *Honey Wheat,* or any of the fruit scones.

SHORTCAKE

Try strawberry shortcake using *Traditional, Honey Wheat* or *Lemon* scones. Use the triangular-shaped scones, or, if you like, change the scones to round by rolling dough into a log, 6 inches thick and cutting 1-inch slices off it.

BASIC GLAZE

Almost all of the recipes in this book can be made as they are or with one of the following sweet glazes. Each recipe suggests the glazes that best complement each scone.

$\frac{1}{2}$ cup confectioners' sugar
2–2$\frac{1}{2}$ tsp. hot water

Combine sugar and 2 tsp. hot water, making sure there are no lumps. If a thinner glaze is desired add hot water by $\frac{1}{4}$ tsp. until desired consistency is reached.

VANILLA, MAPLE OR COCONUT GLAZE

Add $\frac{1}{8}$ tsp. vanilla, maple or coconut extract to *Basic Glaze* recipe.

LEMON OR ORANGE GLAZE

Add $\frac{1}{4}$ tsp. finely grated lemon or orange zest (only the yellow or orange part) and $\frac{1}{8}$ tsp. lemon or orange extract to *Basic Glaze* recipe.

TRADITIONAL SCONES

This is a good basic scone recipe. Feel free to substitute other dried fruit or add ½ to ¾ cup finely chopped nuts (toasted almonds, hazelnuts, pecans, etc.) to vary the recipe. Serve with jam or butter.

1¾ cup all-purpose flour
¼ cup sugar
2½ tsp. baking powder
¼ tsp. salt
6 tbs. unsalted butter, chilled

½ cup dried currants
1 egg
¼ cup half-and-half
Basic, Vanilla, or *Lemon Glaze,*
  page 7, optional

Heat oven to 375°. Combine flour, sugar, baking powder, and salt until thoroughly blended. Slice butter into flour mixture, making sure each piece is coated with mixture. Using a pastry blender or wire whisk, press into butter (as if you are mashing potatoes) until mixture has a sandy texture resembling fine crumbs. Add currants and make sure they are well blended.

In a separate bowl, beat egg and add half-and-half. Combine egg and flour mixtures using a spoon and then your hands, just until blended. Roll dough into a 12-inch log.

Using your hands or a rolling pin, flatten log into a rectangle measuring 3 x 12 inches and $\frac{1}{2}$- to $\frac{3}{4}$-inch thick. Make sure thickness is consistent throughout dough. Cut rectangle into 4 equal squares and cut each square in half diagonally, making 8 scones.

Evenly space scones on an ungreased cookie sheet. Bake for 15 to 20 minutes, or until scones are firm and bottoms are lightly browned. Coat with glaze if desired.

VARIATIONS

Replace dried currants with roughly chopped dried cranberries, flavored Craisins, or dried cherries.

APPLE SCONES

Cardamom, rather than traditional cinnamon, blends well with the apples to give these scones a unique taste.

1 large apple
1¾ cups + 1 tbs. all-purpose
   flour
2½ tsp. baking powder
¼ tsp. salt
½ cup sugar

3 tsp. cardamom
6 tbs. unsalted butter, chilled
1 egg
¼ cup half-and-half
Basic, Vanilla, or *Lemon Glaze,*
   page 7, optional

Heat oven to 375°. Peel, core, and thinly slice apple, then cut each slice into slivers. Using paper towels, blot all excess moisture. Combine flour, baking powder, salt, sugar and cardamom. Stir well. Slice butter into flour mixture, making sure each piece is coated with mixture. Using a pastry blender or wire whisk, press into butter (as if you are mashing potatoes) until mixture has a sandy texture resembling fine crumbs.

In a separate bowl, beat egg. Add half-and-half and blend well. Combine egg and flour mixtures using a spoon and then your hands, just until blended.

Using a rolling pin, roll dough into a 9 x 12-inch rectangle. Sprinkle apples evenly on dough and press in lightly. Roll dough into a 12-inch log. Using your hands or a rolling pin, flatten the log into a rectangle measuring 3 x 12 inches and $\frac{1}{2}$- to $\frac{3}{4}$-inch thick. Make sure thickness is consistent throughout dough. Cut rectangle into 4 equal squares and cut each square in half diagonally, making 8 scones.

Evenly space scones on an ungreased cookie sheet. Bake for 15 to 20 minutes, or until scones are firm and bottoms are lightly browned. Coat with glaze if desired.

VARIATIONS

Replace apples with firm sweet pears.

APRICOT OAT SCONES

The addition of oats in these scones changes the texture. Apricots give them an added sweetness.

1 1/4 cups + 2 tbs. all-purpose
    flour
1/2 cup oatmeal (quick-cooking)
1/2 cup sugar
2 1/2 tsp. baking powder
1/4 tsp. salt

6 tbs. unsalted butter, chilled
1 egg
1/4 cup half-and-half
1 tsp. vanilla extract
Basic or *Vanilla Glaze,* page 7,
    optional

Heat oven to 375°. Combine flour, oatmeal, sugar, baking powder and salt, until thoroughly blended. Slice butter into flour mixture, making sure each piece is coated with mixture. Using a pastry blender or a wire whisk, press into butter (as if you are mashing potatoes) until mixture has a sandy texture resembling fine crumbs.

In a separate bowl, beat egg. Add half-and-half and vanilla. Blend well. Combine egg and flour mixtures using a spoon and then your hands, just until blended. The batter will be sticky, so place in refrigerator for a half hour so liquid can be absorbed and dough will be easier to work with.

Using a rolling pin, roll dough into a 9 x 12-inch rectangle. Using your hands or a rolling pin, flatten log into a rectangle measuring 3 x 12 inches and $1/2$- to $3/4$-inch thick. Make sure thickness is consistent throughout dough. Cut rectangle into 4 equal squares and cut each square in half diagonally, making 8 scones.

Evenly space scones on an ungreased cookie sheet. Bake for 15 to 20 minutes, or until scones are firm and bottoms are lightly browned. Coat with glaze if desired.

APRICOT PEACH SCONES

Dried apricots and fresh peaches give these scones a burst of flavor and a variety of textures.

1 small firm peach
1³⁄₄ cups + 2 tbs. all-purpose
   flour
¹⁄₂ cup sugar
2¹⁄₂ tsp. baking powder
¹⁄₄ tsp. salt
1 egg

6 tbs. unsalted butter, chilled
¹⁄₄ cup half-and-half
1 tsp. vanilla extract
¹⁄₂ cup finely chopped dried
   apricots
Basic or *Vanilla Glaze,* page 7,
   optional

Heat oven to 375°. Peel, pit, and chop peach into slivers. Place slivers on a paper towel and cover to remove excess moisture.

Combine flour, sugar, baking powder and salt. Stir well. Slice butter and cut into flour mixture, making sure each piece is coated with mixture.

Using a pastry blender or wire whisk, press into butter (as if you are mashing potatoes) until mixture has a sandy texture resembling fine crumbs. In a separate bowl, beat egg. Add half-and-half and vanilla extract. Blend well. Combine egg and flour mixtures just until blended, using a spoon and then your hands.

Using a rolling pin, roll dough into a 12 x 9-inch rectangle. Sprinkle peaches and apricots onto dough and lightly pat down. Roll dough to form a 12-inch log. Using your hands or a rolling pin, flatten log into a rectangle measuring 3 x 12 inches and $\frac{1}{2}$- to $\frac{3}{4}$-inch thick. Make sure thickness is consistent throughout dough. Cut rectangle into 4 equal squares and cut each square in half diagonally, making 8 scones.

Arrange scones on a dry cookie sheet so they are evenly spaced. Bake for 15 to 20 minutes, or until scones are firm and bottoms are lightly browned. Coat with glaze if desired.

BANANA NUT SCONES

Think banana bread with a hearty texture. Make sure the bananas are neither green, nor over-ripe.

½ cup chopped walnuts or
   pecans
1 large ripe banana
1¾ cups + 1 tbs. all-purpose
   flour
½ cup sugar
2½ tsp. baking powder
¼ tsp. salt

6 tbs. unsalted butter, chilled
1 egg
¼ cup half-and-half
1 tsp. vanilla extract
1 egg
Basic or *Vanilla Glaze*, page 7,
   optional

Heat oven to 375°. Place nuts on a dry cookie sheet and bake for 5 minutes. Allow nuts to completely cool before mixing them in the dough Peel, banana and cut into ¼-inch slices. Cut each slice into fourths. Using paper towels, gently blot all excess moisture from bananas.

Combine flour, sugar, baking powder and salt until thoroughly blended. Slice butter into flour mixture, making sure each piece is coated with mixture. Using a pastry blender or wire whisk, press into the butter (as if you are mashing potatoes) until mixture has a sandy texture resembling fine crumbs.

In a separate bowl, beat egg. Add half-and-half and vanilla. Blend well. Combine egg and flour mixtures using a spoon and then your hands, just until blended.

Using a rolling pin, roll dough into a 12 x 9-inch rectangle. Sprinkle bananas onto dough, distributing evenly, and lightly pat down. Roll dough to form a 12-inch log. Using a rolling pin or your hands, flatten log to make a 12 x 3-inch rectangle. Cut rectangle into 4 equal squares and cut each square in half diagonally, making 8 scones. Evenly space scones on an ungreased cookie sheet. Bake for 15 to 20 minutes, or until scones are firm and bottoms are lightly browned. Coat with glaze if desired.

BLACKBERRY SCONES

Blackberries are a very delicate and juicy fruit. Be careful not to crush them when cutting in pieces.

6 oz. blackberries
1¾ cups all-purpose flour
½ cup sugar
2½ tsp. baking powder
¼ tsp. salt
6 tbs. unsalted butter, chilled

1 egg
¼ cup half-and-half
1½ tsp. vanilla extract
Basic, Vanilla, or *Lemon Glaze,*
    page 7, optional

Heat oven to 375°. Cut each blackberry into 2 or 3 slices. Place between paper towels and pat lightly to remove excess moisture. Use additional paper towels if necessary.

Combine flour, sugar, baking powder and salt until thoroughly blended. Slice butter into flour mixture, making sure each piece is coated with mixture. Using a pastry blender or wire whisk, press into the butter (as if you are mashing potatoes) until mixture has a sandy texture resembling fine crumbs.

In a separate bowl, beat egg. Add half-and-half and vanilla. Blend well. Combine egg and flour mixtures using a spoon then your hands, just until blended.

Using a rolling pin, roll dough into a 12 x 9-inch rectangle. Sprinkle berries on dough and lightly pat down. Roll dough to form a 12-inch log. Using your hands or a rolling pin flatten log to make a 12 x 3-inch rectangle about $1/2$- to $3/4$-inch thick. Cut the rectangle into 4 equal squares and cut each square in half diagonally, making 8 scones. Evenly space scones on an ungreased cookie sheet. Bake for 15 to 20 minutes, or until scones are firm and bottoms are lightly browned. Coat with glaze if desired.

VARIATIONS

Try other berries, e.g., strawberries cut into raisin-sized chunks, blue berries, etc. in place of blackberries; or combine more than one type of berry.

CHERRY VANILLA SCONES

Fresh cherries and vanilla create a seasonal favorite.

¾ cup cherries, pitted and cut
   into raisin-sized chunks
1¾ cups all-purpose flour
½ cup sugar
2 tsp. baking powder
¼ tsp. salt

6 tbs. unsalted butter, chilled
1 egg
¼ cup half-and-half
1 tsp. vanilla extract
Basic or *Vanilla Glaze,* page 7,
   optional

Heat oven to 375°. Place cherries between paper towels and lightly pat to remove excess liquid. Set aside.

Combine flour, sugar, baking powder and salt. Stir well. Slice butter into flour mixture, making sure each piece is coated with mixture. Using a pastry blender or wire whisk, press into butter (as if you are mashing potatoes) until mixture has a sandy texture resembling fine crumbs.

In a separate bowl, beat egg. Add half-and-half and vanilla extract. Blend well. Combine egg and flour mixtures just until blended, using a spoon and then your hands.

Using a rolling pin, roll dough into a 9 x 12-inch rectangle. Sprinkle cherries evenly on dough and lightly press down. Roll dough to form a 12-inch log. Flatten log to make a 12 x 3-inch rectangle measuring about $\frac{1}{2}$- to $\frac{3}{4}$-inch thick. Cut rectangle into 4 equal squares and cut each square in half diagonally, making 8 scones.

Arrange scones on a dry cookie sheet so they are evenly spaced. Bake for 15 to 20 minutes, or until scones are firm and bottoms are lightly browned. Coat with glaze if desired.

CINNAMON RAISIN SCONES

If you love cinnamon raisin toast, you'll love this recipe.

1¾ cups all-purpose flour
¾ cup sugar
2½ tsp. baking powder
¼ tsp. salt
2 tsp. cinnamon
6 tbs. unsalted butter, chilled

½ cup raisins
1 egg
¼ cup half-and-half
Basic, Vanilla, or *Lemon Glaze,*
   page 7, optional

Heat oven to 375°. Combine flour, sugar, baking powder, salt and cinnamon.

Slice butter into flour mixture, making sure each piece is coated with mixture. Using a pastry blender or wire whisk, press into butter (as if you are mashing potatoes) until mixture has a sandy texture resembling fine crumbs. Add raisins and blend well.

In a separate bowl, beat egg and blend in half-and-half. Combine egg and flour mixtures just until blended, using a spoon and then your hands.

Roll dough into a 12-inch log. Using your hands or a rolling pin, flatten the log into a rectangle measuring 3 x 12-inches and $1/2$- to $3/4$-inch thick. Make sure thickness is consistent throughout dough. Cut rectangle into 4 equal squares and cut each square in half diagonally, making 8 scones.

Evenly space scones on an ungreased cookie sheet. Bake for 15 to 20 minutes, or until scones are firm and bottoms are lightly browned. Coat with glaze if desired.

LEMON SCONES

These scones have a tart lemon flavor which can be enhanced by lemon glaze. Although poppy seeds were suggested to vary recipe, golden raisins and other dried fruit can be added as well.

1¾ cups all-purpose flour
½ cup sugar
2½ tsp. baking powder
¼ tsp. salt
6 tbs. unsalted butter, chilled
1 egg
⅛ cup half-and-half

⅛ cup lemon juice
1 tsp. lemon extract
3 tsp. fresh-grated lemon peel
   (zest), firmly packed
Basic, Vanilla, or *Lemon Glaze,*
   page 7, optional

Heat oven to 375°. Combine flour, sugar, baking powder, and salt until thoroughly blended. Slice butter into flour mixture, making sure each piece is coated with mixture. Using a pastry blender or wire whisk, press into butter (as if you are mashing potatoes) until mixture has a sandy texture resembling fine crumbs.

In a separate bowl, beat egg. Add in half-and-half, lemon juice, lemon extract, and lemon zest. Combine egg and flour mixture using a spoon and then your hands, just until all ingredients are blended in.

Roll dough into a 12-inch log. Using your hands or a rolling pin, flatten log into a rectangle measuring 3 x 12 inches and $1/2$- to $3/4$-inch thick. Make sure thickness is consistent throughout dough. Cut rectangle into 4 equal squares and cut each square in half diagonally, making 8 scones.

Evenly space scones on an ungreased cookie sheet. Bake for 15 to 20 minutes, or until scones are firm and bottoms are lightly browned. Coat with glaze if desired.

LEMON POPPY SEED SCONES

Follow directions for lemon scones and add 2 tbs. poppy seeds after butter is cut into flour mixture.

LEMON RAISIN POPPY SEED

Add $1/2$ cup golden raisins after poppy seeds.

MANGO MANGO SCONES

Mango juice and dried mango slices make these scones doubly good.

5–6 oz. dried mango slices
1¾ cups all-purpose flour
½ cup sugar
2½ tsp. baking powder
¼ tsp. salt
6 tbs. unsalted butter, chilled

1 egg
¼ cup mango juice
1 tbs. heavy cream.
Basic, Vanilla, Orange, or *Lemon
     Glaze,* page 7, optional

Heat oven to 375°. Stack mango slices on top of each other. Make 1 slice lengthwise, then cut across making ¼-inch slices. This should equal about 1 cup.

Combine flour, sugar, baking powder and salt. Stir well. Slice butter into flour mixture, making sure each piece is coated with mixture. Using a pastry blender or wire whisk, press into butter (as if you are mashing potatoes) until mixture has a sandy texture resembling fine crumbs. Add mangos to flour mixture.

In a separate bowl, beat egg. Add mango juice and cream. Blend well. Combine egg and flour mixtures using a spoon and then your hands, just until blended. Roll dough into a 12-inch log. Using your hands or a rolling pin, flatten log into a rectangle measuring 3 x 12 inches and $\frac{1}{2}$- to $\frac{3}{4}$-inch thick. Make sure thickness is consistent throughout dough. Cut rectangle into 4 equal squares and cut each square in half diagonally, making 8 scones.

Evenly space scones on an ungreased cookie sheet. Bake for 15 to 20 minutes, or until scones are firm and bottoms are lightly browned. Coat with glaze if desired.

ORANGE PINEAPPLE SCONES

The tart flavor of oranges works well with the sweetness of pineapple. Also try substituting cranberries for pineapples.

1¾ cups all-purpose flour
¼ cup sugar
2½ tsp. baking powder
¼ tsp. salt
6 tbs. unsalted butter, chilled
¾ cup dried pineapple, cut into raisin-sized chunks
1 egg

⅛ cup orange juice
⅛ cup half-and-half
3 tsp. finely grated orange peel (zest)
1 tsp. orange extract
Basic, Vanilla, or *Orange Glaze,* page 7, optional

Heat oven to 375°. Combine flour, sugar, baking powder, and salt until thoroughly blended. Slice butter into flour mixture, making sure each piece is coated with mixture. Using a pastry blender or wire whisk, press into butter (as if you are mashing potatoes) until mixture has a sandy texture resembling fine crumbs. Add pineapple.

In a separate bowl, beat egg. Add in juice, rind, and extract. Combine egg and flour mixture using a spoon and then your hands, just until blended.

Roll dough into a 12-inch log. Using your hands or a rolling pin, flatten log into a rectangle measuring 3 x 12 inches and $\frac{1}{2}$- to $\frac{3}{4}$-inch thick. Make sure thickness is consistent throughout dough. Cut rectangle into 4 equal squares and cut each square in half diagonally, making 8 scones.

Evenly space scones on an ungreased cookie sheet. Bake for 15 to 20 minutes, or until scones are firm and bottoms are lightly browned. Coat with glaze if desired.

ORANGE CRANBERRY SCONES

Substitute roughly chopped dried cranberries or Craisins for dried pineapple.

RAISIN GINGER BREAD SCONES

The flavor of these scones is a combination of ginger bread and ginger snaps. If you prefer a milder flavor, reduce ginger to 1 or $1/2$ teaspoon.

$1^3/4$ cups + 1 tbs. all-purpose
   flour
$1/4$ cup brown sugar
$1/4$ cup sugar
$2^1/2$ tsp. baking powder
$1/4$ tsp. salt
$1/2$ tsp. cinnamon

$1^1/2$ tsp. ground ginger
6 tbs. unsalted butter, chilled
$3/4$ cup raisins
1 egg
$1/4$ cup half-and-half
Basic, Vanilla, or *Lemon Glaze,*
   page 7, optional

Heat oven to 375°. Combine flour, sugars, baking powder, salt, cinnamon, and ginger. Slice butter into flour mixture, making sure each piece is coated with mixture. Using a pastry blender or wire whisk, press into butter (as if you are mashing potatoes) until mixture has a sandy texture resembling fine crumbs.

Add raisins and blend well.

In a separate bowl, beat egg and blend in half-and-half. Combine egg and flour mixtures using a spoon and then your hands, just until blended.

Roll dough into a 12-inch log. Using your hands or a rolling pin, flatten the log into a rectangle measuring 3 x 12 inches and $1/2$- to $3/4$-inch thick. Make sure thickness is consistent throughout dough. Cut rectangle into 4 equal squares and cut each square in half diagonally, making 8 scones.

Evenly space scones on an ungreased cookie sheet. Bake for 15 to 20 minutes, or until scones are firm and bottoms are lightly browned. Coat with glaze if desired.

RASPBERRY SCONES

My colleague TJ, a self-professed "southern girl" was sure that scones would be too close to biscuits and she wouldn't like them. This is the recipe that changed her mind.

6 oz. raspberries
1¾ cups all-purpose flour
½ cup sugar
2½ tsp. baking powder
¼ tsp. salt
6 tbs. unsalted butter, chilled

1 egg
¼ cup half-and-half
1½ tsp. raspberry extract
Basic, Vanilla, or *Lemon Glaze,*
   page 7, optional

Heat oven to 375°. Place raspberries between paper towels and pat lightly to remove excess moisture. Use additional paper towels if necessary.

Combine flour, sugar, baking powder, and salt until thoroughly blended. Slice butter into flour mixture, making sure each piece is coated with mixture.

Using a pastry blender or wire whisk, press into butter (as if you are mashing potatoes) until mixture has a sandy texture resembling fine crumbs.

In a separate bowl, beat egg. Add in half-and-half and extract. Combine egg and flour mixture using a spoon and then your hands, just until all ingredients are blended in.

Using a rolling pin, roll dough into a 9 x 12-inch rectangle. Sprinkle raspberries evenly on to dough and lightly pat down. Roll dough into a 12-inch log. Using your hands or a rolling pin, flatten log into a rectangle measuring 3 x 12 inches and $\frac{1}{2}$- to $\frac{3}{4}$-inch thick. Make sure thickness is consistent throughout dough. Cut rectangle into 4 equal squares and cut each square in half diagonally, making 8 scones.

Evenly space scones on an ungreased cookie sheet. Bake for 15 to 20 minutes, or until scones are firm and bottoms are lightly browned. Coat with glaze if desired.

TUTTI FRUTTI SCONES

Tutti Frutti in Italian means "all fruit." Select any combination of dried fruits to equal 1 cup. Berries and pineapple are especially good.

1¾ cups all-purpose flour
¼ cup sugar
2½ tsp. baking powder
¼ tsp. salt
6 tbs. unsalted butter, chilled
1 cup mixed finely chopped
  dried fruits (berries,

pineapples, apricots, mangos,
  cherries, etc.)
1 egg
¼ cup half-and-half
1 tsp. raspberry extract
Basic, Vanilla, or *Lemon Glaze,*
  page 7, optional

Heat oven to 375°. Combine flour, sugar, baking powder, and salt until thoroughly blended. Slice butter into flour mixture, making sure each piece is coated with mixture. Using a pastry blender or wire whisk, press into butter (as if you are mashing potatoes) until mixture has a sandy texture resembling fine crumbs.

Add fruits and make sure they are well blended. In a separate bowl, beat egg and add in half-and-half. Combine egg and flour mixtures using a spoon and then your hands, just until blended.

Roll dough into a 12-inch log. Using your hands or a rolling pin, flatten log into a rectangle measuring 3 x 12 inches and $\frac{1}{2}$- to $\frac{3}{4}$-inch thick. Make sure thickness is consistent throughout dough. Cut rectangle into 4 equal squares and cut each square in half diagonally, making 8 scones.

Evenly space scones on an ungreased cookie sheet. Bake for 15 to 20 minutes, or until scones are firm and bottoms are lightly browned. Coat with glaze if desired.

VARIATIONS

Replace dried currants with roughly chopped dried cranberries, flavored Craisins, or dried cherries.

CARROT SCONES

Think of carrot cake in a scone. If you prefer spicier, add another ½ teaspoon cinnamon, ¼ teaspoon nutmeg, and ¼ teaspoon allspice.

½ cup finely chopped walnuts
½ cup carrots, peeled and
   finely grated
1¾ cups all-purpose flour
½ cup sugar
2½ tsp. baking powder
¼ tsp. salt
1½ tsp. cinnamon

1 tsp. nutmeg
½ tsp. allspice
6 tbs. unsalted butter, chilled
1 egg
¼ cup half-and-half
Basic or *Vanilla Glaze*, page 7,
   optional

Heat oven to 375°. Place nuts on a dry cookie sheet and bake for 5 minutes. Make sure nuts are cool before adding to dough.

Squeeze all moisture from carrots, then tightly wrap them in a paper towel to remove any remaining moisture. Set aside. Combine flour, sugar, baking powder, salt, cinnamon, nutmeg, and allspice.

Slice butter into flour mixture, making sure each piece is coated with mixture. Using a pastry blender or wire whisk, press into butter (as if you are mashing potatoes) until mixture has a sandy texture resembling fine crumbs. Add walnuts and blend in.

In a separate bowl, beat egg. Add in half-and-half and carrots. Combine egg/carrot mixture and flour mixture, first mixing with a spoon, then your hands.

Roll dough into a 12-inch log. Using your hands or a rolling pin, flatten log into a rectangle measuring 3 x 12 inches by $1/2$- to $3/4$-inch thick. Make sure thickness is consistent throughout dough. Cut rectangle into 4 equal squares and cut each square in half diagonally, making 8 scones. Evenly space scones on an ungreased cookie sheet. Bake for 15 to 20 minutes, or until scones are firm and bottoms are lightly browned. Coat with glaze if desired.

DRIED FRUIT AND CARROT SCONES

Add raisins or dried pineapple cut into raisin-sized chunks, along with nuts. Change walnuts to pecans.

DATE AND NUT SCONES

Date and nut bread was the inspiration for these scones. They have a mild flavor enhanced by the brown sugar.

1/2 cup chopped walnuts or
    pecans
1 3/4 cups + 1 tbs. all-purpose
    flour
1/2 cup brown sugar, firmly
    packed
2 1/2 tsp. baking powder
1/4 tsp. salt

6 tbs. unsalted butter, chilled
1 cup dried dates
1 egg
1/4 cup half-and-half
1 tsp. vanilla extract
Basic or *Vanilla Glaze,* page 7,
    optional

Heat oven to 375°. Place nuts on a dry cookie sheet and bake for 5 minutes. Make sure nuts are cool before adding to dough.

Combine flour, sugar, baking powder, and salt until thoroughly blended. Slice butter into flour mixture, making sure each piece is coated with mixture. Using a pastry blender or wire whisk, press into butter (as if you are mashing potatoes) until mixture has a sandy texture resembling fine crumbs. Cut each date lengthwise in fourths, then cut across 2 or 3 times Add dates and walnuts. Blend well.

In a separate bowl, beat egg. Add in half-and-half and vanilla. Combine egg and flour mixtures using a spoon then your hands, just until all ingredients are blended.

Roll dough into a 12-inch log. Using your hands or a rolling pin, flatten log into a rectangle measuring 3 x 12-inches and $\frac{1}{2}$- to $\frac{3}{4}$-inch thick. Make sure thickness is consistent throughout dough. Cut rectangle into 4 equal squares and cut each square in half diagonally, making 8 scones.

Evenly space scones on an ungreased cookie sheet. Bake for 15 to 20 minutes, or until scones are firm and bottoms are lightly browned. Coat with glaze if desired.

ALMOND JOY SCONES

As the name implies, these scones are flavored with chocolate, coconut and almonds, reminiscent of a favorite childhood candy bar.

1¾ cups all-purpose flour
½ cup sugar
2½ tsp. baking powder
¼ tsp. salt
6 tbs. unsalted butter, chilled
¾ cup sweetened coconut
  flakes
¾ cup chocolate mini chips
½ cup chopped toasted
  almonds
1 egg
¼ cup half-and-half
2 tsp. coconut extract
Basic, Vanilla, or *Coconut Glaze,*
  page 7, optional

Heat oven to 375°. Combine flour, sugar, baking powder, and salt until thoroughly blended. Slice butter into flour mixture, making sure each piece is coated with mixture.

Using a pastry blender or wire whisk, press into butter (as if you are mashing potatoes) until mixture has a sandy texture resembling fine crumbs. Add coconut, chips, and almonds. Blend well.

In a separate bowl, beat egg and add in half-and-half and coconut extract. Combine egg and flour mixtures just until all ingredients are blended, first with a spoon and then with your hands.

Roll dough into a 12-inch log. Using your hands or a rolling pin, flatten log into a rectangle measuring 3 x 12 inches and $1/2$- to $3/4$-inches thick. Make sure thickness is consistent throughout dough. Cut rectangle into 4 equal squares and cut each square in half diagonally, making 8 scones.

Evenly space scones on an ungreased cookie sheet. Bake for 15 to 20 minutes, or until scones are firm and bottoms are lightly browned. Coat with glaze if desired.

BUTTER PECAN SCONES

The inspiration for these scones was butter pecan ice cream. Butter and vanilla extracts bring out the buttery goodness of the pecans.

¾ cup finely chopped pecans
1¾ cups all-purpose flour
½ cup sugar
2½ tsp. baking powder
¼ tsp. salt
6 tbs. unsalted butter, chilled

1 egg
¼ cup half-and-half
1 tsp. vanilla extract
½ tsp. butter flavored extract
Basic or *Vanilla Glaze*, page 7, optional

Heat oven to 375°. Place pecans on a cookie sheet and bake for 5 to 10 minutes. Make sure they are cool before adding to dough.

Combine flour, sugar, baking powder, and salt until thoroughly blended. Slice butter into flour mixture, making sure each piece is coated with mixture.

Using a pastry blender or wire whisk, press into butter (as if you are mashing potatoes) until mixture has a sandy texture resembling fine crumbs. Add pecans and blend well.

Beat egg and add half-and-half, vanilla, and butter extracts. Combine egg and flour mixture, first with a spoon then your hands, just until all ingredients are blended in.

Roll dough into a 12-inch log. Using your hands or a rolling pin, flatten log into a rectangle measuring 3 x 12 inches and $1/2$- to $3/4$-inch thick. Make sure thickness is consistent throughout dough. Cut rectangle into 4 equal squares and cut each square in half diagonally, making 8 scones.

Evenly space scones on an ungreased cookie sheet. Bake for 15 to 20 minutes, or until scones are firm and bottoms are lightly browned. Coat with glaze if desired.

BUTTERSCOTCH MAPLE NUT SCONES

These scones are great for a sweet tooth. They have a rich dense texture and butterscotch flavor. Add maple glaze for an even sweeter scone.

1¾ cups + 1 tbs. all-purpose flour
¼ cup brown sugar
¼ cup sugar
2½ tsp. baking powder
¼ tsp. salt
6 tbs. unsalted butter, chilled
1 cup butterscotch chips

½ cup finely chopped walnuts or pecans
1 egg
¼ cup half-and-half
½ tsp. maple extract
Basic, Vanilla, or *Maple Glaze,* page 7, optional

Heat oven to 375°. Place nuts on a dry cookie sheet and bake for 5 minutes. Allow nuts to completely cool before mixing them in dough.

Combine flour, sugars, baking powder, and salt until thoroughly blended. Slice butter into flour mixture, making sure each piece is coated with mixture. Using a pastry blender or wire whisk, press into butter (as if you are mashing potatoes) until mixture has a sandy texture resembling fine crumbs. Add chips and make sure they are evenly distributed.

In a separate bowl, beat egg and add in half-and-half and maple extract. Combine egg and flour mixtures just until all ingredients are blended, first with a spoon and then with your hands.

Roll dough into a 12-inch log. Using your hands or a rolling pin, flatten log into a rectangle measuring 6 x 12 inches and $1/2$- to $3/4$-inch thick. Make sure thickness is consistent throughout dough. Cut rectangle into 4 equal squares and cut each square in half diagonally, making 8 scones. Evenly space scones on an ungreased cookie sheet. Bake for 15 to 20 minutes, or until scones are firm and bottoms are lightly browned. Coat with glaze if desired.

CHOCOLATE CHIP SCONES

These scones taste like soft chocolate chip cookies. To vary them, substitute ³/4 cup white or milk chocolate chips.

½ cup finely chopped walnuts
1¾ cups + 1 tbs. all-purpose
   flour
¼ cup sugar
¼ cup brown sugar
2½ tsp. baking powder
¼ tsp. salt

6 tbs. unsalted butter, chilled
³/4 cup mini chocolate chips
1 egg
¼ cup half-and-half
1 tsp. vanilla extract
Basic or *Vanilla Glaze,* page 7,
   optional

Heat oven to 375°. Place nuts on a dry cookie sheet and bake for 5 minutes. Allow nuts to completely cool before mixing them in the dough.

Combine flour, sugars, baking powder, and salt until thoroughly blended. Slice butter into flour mixture, making sure each piece is coated with mixture.

Using a pastry blender or wire whisk, press into butter (as if you are mashing potatoes) until mixture has a sandy texture resembling fine crumbs. Add chips and walnuts and blend well.

Beat egg and add in half-and-half and vanilla. Combine egg and flour mixtures just until all ingredients are blended, first using a spoon and then with your hands.

Roll dough into a 12-inch log. Using your hands or a rolling pin, flatten log into a rectangle measuring 3 x 12 inches and $\frac{1}{2}$- to $\frac{3}{4}$-inch thick. Make sure thickness is consistent throughout dough. Cut rectangle into 4 equal squares and cut each square in half diagonally, making 8 scones. Evenly space scones on an ungreased cookie sheet. Bake for 15 to 20 minutes, or until scones are firm and bottoms are lightly browned. Coat with glaze if desired.

PECAN- OR ALL-CHOCOLATE-CHIP SCONES

Replace walnuts with pecans, or hazelnuts or leave out nuts all together. Replace chocolate chips with white chocolate chips.

CHOCOLATE HAZELNUT SCONES

Toast hazelnuts by placing them in the oven at 400° for 10 to 15 minutes, until golden brown. Be careful not to burn. Remove from oven, wrap in a dish towel and rub together until most skins are off.

1¾ cups all-purpose flour
2½ tsp. baking powder
¼ tsp. salt
½ cup sugar
2 tbs. cocoa (Dutch processed)
6 tbs. unsalted butter, chilled

1 cup finely chopped toasted
    unsalted hazelnuts
1 egg
¼ cup half-and-half
1 tsp. vanilla extract
Basic or *Vanilla Glaze*, page 7,
    optional

Heat oven to 375°. Combine flour, baking powder, salt, sugar, and cocoa until thoroughly blended. Slice butter into flour mixture, making sure each piece is coated with mixture. Using a pastry blender or wire whisk, press into butter (as if you are mashing potatoes) until mixture has a sandy texture resembling fine crumbs.

Add hazelnuts and blend well. Beat egg and add in half-and-half, and vanilla extract. Combine flour and egg mixtures using a spoon then your hands just until ingredients are blended together. Roll dough into a 12-inch log. Using your hands or a rolling pin, flatten log into a rectangle measuring about 3 x 12 inches and $3/4$-inch thick. Make sure thickness is consistent throughout dough. Cut rectangle into 4 equal squares and cut each square in half diagonally, making 8 scones.

Evenly space scones on an ungreased cookie sheet. Bake for 15 to 20 minutes, or until scones are firm and bottoms are lightly browned. Coat with glaze if desired.

HAZELNUT CHOCOLATE CHIP SCONES

Add $1/2$ cup chocolate or white chocolate chips

CHOCOLATE ALMOND SCONES

Replace vanilla extract with $1/2$ tsp. almond extract and replace hazelnuts with roasted, unsalted almonds.

CRANBERRY CASHEW CHIP SCONES

White chocolate chips complement tart cranberries. Cashews add another layer of flavor in this recipe.

1¾ cups all purpose flour
¼ cup sugar
2½ tsp. baking powder
¼ tsp. salt
6 tbs. unsalted butter, chilled
¼ cup white chocolate chips
¾ cup dried sweetened
  cranberries or Craisins

¼ cup chopped, unsalted,
  roasted cashews
1 egg
¼ cup half-and-half
1 tsp. vanilla extract
Basic or *Vanilla Glaze,* page 7,
  optional

Heat oven to 375°. Combine flour, sugar, baking powder and salt. Stir well. Slice butter into flour mixture, making sure each piece is coated with mixture. Using a pastry blender or wire whisk, press into butter (as if you are mashing potatoes) until mixture has a sandy texture resembling fine crumbs.

Add chips, cranberries, and cashews, to flour mixture.

In a separate bowl, beat egg. Add half-and-half and vanilla. Blend well. Combine egg and flour mixtures with a spoon and then your hands, just until blended. Roll dough into a 12-inch log.

Using your hands or a rolling pin, flatten log into a rectangle measuring 3 x 12 inches and $\frac{1}{2}$- to $\frac{3}{4}$-inch thick. Make sure thickness is consistent throughout dough. Cut rectangle into 4 equal squares and cut each square in half diagonally, making 8 scones.

Evenly space scones on an ungreased cookie sheet. Bake for 15 to 20 minutes, or until scones are firm and bottoms are lightly browned. Coat with glaze if desired.

CRANBERRY MACADAMIA CHIP SCONES

Replace cashews with Macadamia nuts.

CHERRY MACADAMIA CHIP SCONES

Replace cranberries with dried cherries.

HAZELNUT SCONES

When toasted, hazelnuts have a sweet smoky flavor. If you prefer another nut, substitute an equal amount.

3/4 cup chopped hazelnuts
1 3/4 cups + 1 tbs. all-purpose
  flour
1/2 cup sugar
2 1/2 tsp. baking powder
1/4 tsp. salt

6 tbs. unsalted butter, chilled
1 egg
1 tsp. vanilla extract
1/4 cup half-and-half
Basic or *Vanilla Glaze*, page 7,
  optional

Heat oven to 375°. Toast hazelnuts on a cookie sheet for 10 to 15 minutes, until golden brown. Be careful not to burn. Remove from oven, wrap in a dish towel and rub together until most skins are off. Make sure nuts are completely cool before adding to dough.

Combine flour, sugar, baking powder, and salt until thoroughly blended. Slice butter into flour mixture, making sure each piece is coated with mixture.

Using a pastry blender or wire whisk, press into butter (as if you are mashing potatoes) until mixture has a sandy texture resembling fine crumbs. Add hazelnuts and blend in. Set aside.

Beat egg and add vanilla and half-and-half. Combine egg and flour mixtures with a spoon and then with your hands, just until blended.

Roll dough into a 12-inch log. Using your hands or a rolling pin, flatten log into a rectangle measuring 3 x 12 inches and ½-inch thick. Make sure thickness is consistent throughout dough. Cut rectangle into 4 equal squares and cut each square in half diagonally, making 8 scones.

Evenly space scones on an ungreased cookie sheet. Bake for 15 to 20 minutes, or until scones are firm and bottoms are lightly browned. Coat with glaze if desired.

MAPLE WALNUT SCONES

Eat these scones for dessert or anytime with tea or coffee. For a change of pace, serve them warm with butter and maple syrup.

1 cup chopped walnuts
1¾ cups all purpose flour
½ cup sugar
2½ tsp. baking powder
¼ tsp. salt
6 tbs. unsalted butter, chilled

1 egg
¼ cup half-and-half
1 tsp. maple extract
½ tsp. vanilla extract
Basic, Maple or *Vanilla Glaze,*
    page 7, optional

Heat oven to 375°. Place nuts on a dry cookie sheet and bake for 5 minutes. Allow nuts to completely cool before mixing them in the dough. Combine flour, sugar, baking powder, salt. Stir well. Slice butter into flour mixture, making sure each piece is coated with mixture.

Using a pastry blender or wire whisk, press into butter (as if you are mashing potatoes) until mixture has a sandy texture resembling fine crumbs. Add walnuts to flour mixture. In a separate bowl, beat egg. Add cream, maple and vanilla extracts and blend well. Combine egg and flour mixtures just until blended, first with a spoon and then with your hands.

Roll dough into a 12-inch log. Using your hands or a rolling pin, flatten log into a rectangle measuring 3 x 12 inches and $\frac{1}{2}$- to $\frac{3}{4}$-inch thick. Make sure thickness is consistent throughout dough. Cut rectangle into 4 equal squares and cut each square in half diagonally, making 8 scones.

Evenly space scones on an ungreased cookie sheet. Bake for 15 to 20 minutes, or until scones are firm and bottoms are lightly browned. Coat with glaze if desired.

MOCHA CHIP SCONES

Just a hint of coffee enhances the chocolate flavor. If you desire a stronger coffee increase the coffee to 3/4 or 1 teaspoon.

1¾ cups all-purpose flour
¼ cup sugar
¼ cup brown sugar
2½ tsp. baking powder
¼ tsp. salt
½ tbs. cocoa
½ tsp. instant coffee

6 tbs. unsalted butter, chilled
1 cup chocolate mini chips
1 egg
¼ cup half-and-half
1 tsp. vanilla extract
Basic or *Vanilla Glaze,* page 7, optional

Heat oven to 375°. Combine flour, sugar, baking powder, salt, cocoa, and coffee until thoroughly blended. Slice butter into flour mixture using a pastry blender or wire whisk until mixture has a sandy texture resembling fine crumbs. Add chips and blend well.

In a separate bowl, beat egg; add in half-and-half and vanilla.

Combine egg and flour mixture just until all ingredients are blended, first with a spoon and then with your hand.

Roll dough into a 12-inch log. Using your hands or a rolling pin, flatten log into a rectangle measuring 3 x 12 inches and $1/2$- to $3/4$-inch thick. Make sure thickness is consistent throughout dough. Cut rectangle into 4 equal squares and cut each square in half diagonally, making 8 scones.

Evenly space scones on an ungreased cookie sheet. Bake for 15 to 20 minutes, or until scones are firm and bottoms are lightly browned. Coat with glaze if desired.

VARIATIONS

Add 1 to 2 tsp. of coffee or cocoa to increase the intensity of your preferred flavor.

NUTS ABOUT SCONES

This is a great recipe for odd bits of leftover nuts. Mix and match them in any combination to equal 1 cup. I recommend almonds, pistachios, brazil nuts, macadamias, walnuts, pecans or cashews.

1 cup finely chopped, mixed, toasted unsalted nuts
1¾ cups + 1 tbs. all-purpose flour
½ cup sugar
2½ tsp. baking powder
¼ tsp. salt

6 tbs. unsalted butter, chilled
1 egg
1 tsp. vanilla extract
½ tsp. butter flavored extract
¼ cup half-and-half
Basic or *Vanilla Glaze,* page 7, optional

Heat oven to 375°. Toast nuts on a cookie sheet until golden brown. Be careful not to burn. Remove from oven. If toasting hazelnuts, wrap in a dish towel and rub together until most skins are off. Make sure nuts are completely cool before adding to dough.

Combine flour, sugar, baking powder and salt until thoroughly blended. Slice butter into flour mixture, making sure each piece is coated with mixture. Using a pastry blender or wire whisk, press into butter (as if you are mashing potatoes) until mixture has a sandy texture resembling fine crumbs. Add nuts and blend in.

In a separate bowl, beat egg and add in half-and-half. Combine egg and flour mixtures with a spoon and then your hands, just until blended.

Roll dough into a 12-inch log. Using your hands or a rolling pin, flatten log into a rectangle measuring 3 x 12 inches and $\frac{1}{2}$-inch thick. Make sure thickness is consistent throughout dough. Cut rectangle into 4 equal squares and cut each square in half diagonally, making 8 scones.

Evenly space scones on an ungreased cookie sheet. Bake for 15 to 20 minutes, or until scones are firm and bottoms are lightly browned. Coat with glaze if desired.

PEANUT BUTTER SCONES

Instead of butter I used crunchy peanut butter. The result is a dense moist scone, with a peanutty flavor. Try roasted cashew or almond butter for a change of pace.

1½ cups + 1 tbs. all-purpose flour
¼ cup whole wheat flour
¼ tsp. salt
½ cup sugar
2½ tsp. baking powder
9 tbs. crunchy unsalted peanut butter

½ cup chopped roasted unsalted peanuts
1 egg
½ cup half-and-half
Basic or *Vanilla Glaze,* page 7, optional

Heat oven to 375°. Combine flours, salt, sugar, and baking powder until thoroughly blended. Add peanut butter into flour by tablespoons full, covering each spoonful of peanut butter with flour mixture. Using a pastry blender or wire whisk, cut peanut butter into flour until mixture has a sandy texture, similar to fine crumbs. Add chopped peanuts and blend.

In a separate bowl, beat egg and half-and-half. Pour egg mixture into peanut butter mixture and combine just until blended.

Roll dough into a 12-inch log. Using your hands or a rolling pin, flatten log into a rectangle measuring 6 x 12 inches and $1/2$- to $3/4$-inch thick. Make sure thickness is consistent throughout dough. Cut rectangle into 4 equal squares and cut each square in half diagonally, making 8 scones. Evenly space scones on an ungreased cookie sheet. Bake for 15 to 20 minutes, until bottoms are lightly browned. Coat with glaze if desired.

ALMOND BUTTER SCONES

Replace peanut butter with roasted almond butter and peanuts with roasted almonds

CASHEW BUTTER SCONES

Replace peanut butter with cashew butter and peanuts with cashews.

BACON CHEDDAR SCONES

Think Sunday morning breakfast—cheddar cheese omelet and bacon, or a grilled bacon and cheese sandwich. Have these for a quick breakfast on the run or an afternoon snack.

6 strips of thick cut bacon
   (1/3 lb.)
1 3/4 cups all-purpose flour
1/4 tsp. salt
1 tsp. sugar
3 tsp. baking powder
6 tbs. unsalted butter, chilled

1/4 lb. shredded cheddar cheese
1 finely sliced medium scallion
1 egg
1/4 cup half-and-half
1 tsp. bacon fat (room
   temperature)

Heat oven to 375°. Fry bacon until browned but not crispy. Drain well on paper towel. Cut off all excess fat and finely chop bacon. (Should make 1/3 cup.) Reserve 1 tsp. bacon fat. Set bacon and fat aside.

Combine flour, salt, sugar and baking powder. Slice butter into flour mixture, making sure each piece is coated with mixture. Using a pastry blender or wire whisk, press into butter (as if mashing potatoes) until mixture has a sandy texture resembling fine crumbs.

In a separate bowl, beat egg. Add half-and-half and bacon fat. Blend well. Combine egg and flour mixtures just until all ingredients are blended. Add cheese, bacon, and scallion and blend well.

Roll dough into a 12-inch log. Using your hands or a rolling pin, flatten log into a rectangle measuring 3 x 12 inches and ¾-inch thick. Make sure thickness is consistent throughout dough. Cut rectangle into 4 equal squares and cut each square in half diagonally, making 8 scones.

Evenly space scones on an ungreased cookie sheet. Bake for 15 to 20 minutes, until bottoms are lightly browned. Serve warm.

VEGETARIAN BACON AND CHEESE

Replace bacon with vegetarian substitute in recipe.

HAM AND SWISS ON RYE

If you've ever had ham and Swiss on seeded rye, you'll recognize these flavors encased in a scone. Serve with soup or salad.

1¼ cups all purpose flour
½ cup rye flour
3 tsp. baking powder
¼ tsp. salt
6 tbs. unsalted butter, chilled
1 tsp. caraway seeds

¾ cup finely chopped lean ham (4–6 oz.)
¾ cup finely shredded Swiss cheese (4–6 oz.)
1 egg
¼ cup half-and-half

Heat oven to 375°. Combine flours, baking powder, and salt until thoroughly blended. Slice butter into flour mixture, making sure each piece is coated with mixture. Using a pastry blender or wire whisk, press into butter (as if mashing potatoes) until mixture has a sandy texture resembling fine crumbs. Add caraway seeds, ham, and cheese, and blend well.

In a separate bowl, beat egg and add half-and-half. Combine egg and flour mixtures, first with a spoon and then with your hands, just until all ingredients are blended.

Roll dough into a 12-inch log. Using your hands or a rolling pin, flatten log into a rectangle measuring 3 x 12 inches and ¾-inch thick. Make sure thickness is consistent throughout dough. Cut rectangle into 4 equal squares and cut each square in half diagonally, making 8 scones.

Evenly space scones on an ungreased cookie sheet. Bake for 15 to 20 minutes, or until scones are firm and bottoms are lightly browned. Serve warm.

VEGETARIAN HAM AND SWISS ON RYE

Replace ham with vegetarian substitute and proceed with recipe.

HONEY WHEAT

These savory scones have a touch of honey and are slightly sweet. Eat them as you would a biscuit or roll. Serve warm with butter and jelly, in an open-faced sandwich, or split open with melted cheese.

1½ cups all-purpose flour
¼ cup + 1 tbs. whole wheat
   flour
3 tsp. baking powder
¼ tsp. salt
1 tbs. sugar

6 tbs. unsalted butter, chilled
1 egg
¼ cup half-and-half
2 tbs. honey
1 tsp. butter flavored extract

Heat oven to 375°. Combine flours, baking powder, salt, and sugar until thoroughly blended. Slice butter into flour mixture, making sure each piece is coated with mixture. Using a pastry blender or wire whisk, press into the butter (as if mashing potatoes) until mixture has a sandy texture resembling fine crumbs.

In a separate bowl, beat egg. Add half-and-half, honey and butter extract. Combine egg and flour mixtures just until all ingredients are blended.

Roll dough into a 12-inch log. Using your hands or a rolling pin, flatten log into a rectangle measuring 3 x 12 inches and $1/2$- to $3/4$-inch thick. Make sure thickness is consistent throughout dough. Cut rectangle into 4 equal squares and cut each square in half diagonally, making 8 scones.

Evenly space scones on an ungreased cookie sheet. Bake for 15 to 20 minutes, or until scones are firm and bottoms are lightly browned. Serve warm.

JALAPEÑO CORN SCONES

Jalapeño peppers, cheddar cheese and corn meal make this a spicy cornbread in a scone. Try with soup, chili or salad, or in place of toast with your favorite egg dish. Jalapeño peppers leave a very spicy residue on the hands. Be sure to wash your hands thoroughly after preparing them, or do as I do and wear rubber gloves!

1 small jalapeño pepper
1½ cups all purpose flour
¼ cup + 1 tbs. corn meal
¼ tsp. salt
3 tsp. baking powder
1 tbs. sugar

6 tbs. unsalted butter, chilled
1 cup finely grated cheddar
  cheese (about 4 oz.)
1 egg
¼ cup half-and-half
1 tsp. butter flavored extract

Heat oven to 375°. Cut jalapeño in half lengthwise. Scoop out seeds and inner membranes. Finely mince and measure 1 tbs.

Combine flour, corn meal, salt, baking powder and sugar until thoroughly blended.

Slice butter into flour mixture, making sure each piece is coated with mixture. Using a pastry blender or wire whisk, press into butter (as if you are mashing potatoes) until mixture has a sandy texture resembling fine crumbs. Add cheese to flour mixture and blend well.

In a separate bowl, beat egg. Add jalapeños, half-and-half and butter extract. Combine egg and flour mixtures first with a spoon and then your hands, just until all ingredients are blended.

Roll dough into a 12-inch log. Using your hands or a rolling pin, flatten log into a rectangle measuring 3 x 12 inches and $1/2$- to $3/4$-inch thick. Make sure thickness is consistent throughout dough. Cut rectangle into 4 equal squares and cut each square in half diagonally, making 8 scones.

Evenly space scones on an ungreased cookie sheet. Bake for 15 to 20 minutes, or until scones are firm and bottoms are lightly browned. Serve warm.

ONION POPPY SEED SCONES

My inspiration for these scones was a childhood memory of a savory cookie my mother used to make that had poppy seeds and onions, or it may remind you of a poppy seed onion roll from your local bakery.

1¾ cups all-purpose flour
3 tsp. baking powder
¼ tsp. salt
1 tbs. sugar
¼ freshly ground pepper
1 tbs. poppy seeds

6 tbs. unsalted butter, chilled
1 cup finely minced onion
1 egg
¼ cup half-and-half
1 tsp. butter extract

Heat oven to 375°. Combine flour, baking powder, salt, sugar, pepper and poppy seeds until thoroughly blended. Slice butter into flour mixture, making sure each piece is coated with mixture. Using a pastry blender or wire whisk, press into the butter (as if you are mashing potatoes) until mixture has a sandy texture resembling fine crumbs. Add onions and blend into flour mixture.

In a separate bowl, beat egg. Add half-and-half and butter extract. Combine egg and flour mixtures and onions, first mixing with a spoon then your hands, just until all ingredients are blended.

Roll dough into a 12-inch log. Using your hands or a rolling pin, flatten log into a rectangle measuring 3 x 12 inches and ½- to ¾-inch thick. Make sure thickness is consistent throughout dough. Cut the rectangle into 4 equal squares and cut each square in half diagonally, making 8 scones.

Evenly space scones on an ungreased cookie sheet. Bake for 15 to 20 minutes, or until bottoms are lightly browned. Serve warm.

SESAME SCONES

If you want to vary these scones, brush them in egg and roll them in raw sesame seeds before baking. This will give them an added layer of flavor and crunch.

5 tbs. toasted sesame seeds
1½ cups all purpose flour
¼ cup + 1 tbs. whole wheat
  flour
3 tsp. baking powder
¼ tsp. salt

2 tbs. sugar
6 tbs. unsalted butter, chilled
1 egg
¼ cup half-and-half
2 tsp. toasted sesame oil

Heat oven to 375°. Toast sesame seeds by placing them in a thin layer on a cookie sheet for 10 to 15 minutes, making sure they do not burn. Set aside, and make sure they are cool before adding to dough.

Combine flours, baking powder, salt and sugar until thoroughly blended. Slice butter into flour mixture, making sure each piece is coated with mixture. Using a pastry blender or wire whisk, press into butter (as if you are mashing potatoes) until mixture has a sandy texture resembling fine crumbs. Add cooled sesame seeds and blend well.

In a separate bowl, beat egg. Add half-and-half and sesame oil. Combine egg and flour mixtures just until ingredients are blended.

Roll dough into a 12-inch log. Using your hands or a rolling pin, flatten log into a rectangle measuring 3 x 12 inches and $1/2$- to $3/4$-inch thick. Make sure thickness is consistent throughout dough. Cut rectangle into 4 equal squares and cut each square in half diagonally, making 8 scones.

Evenly space scones on an ungreased cookie sheet. Bake for 15 to 20 minutes, or until bottoms are lightly browned. Serve warm.

TOMATO BASIL SCONES

Basil and tomatoes are a natural combination. Try these scones warm with feta or mozzarella cheese and olives.

2 oz. sun-dried tomato (dry, not oil-packed)
1 oz. fresh basil leaves (about ½ cup)
1½ cups all purpose flour
2 tbs. grated Romano (or Parmesan/Romano Cheese)
½ tsp. salt
¼ tsp. freshly ground pepper
3 tsp. baking powder
2 tsp. dehydrated tomato sauce (e.g. McCormick's Thick and Zesty
    Spaghetti Sauce Mix, Lawry's, etc.)
1 tbs. sugar
6 tbs. unsalted butter, chilled
1 egg
¼ cup half-and-half

NOT YOUR GRANNY'S SCONES

Heat oven to 375°. Break sun-dried tomatoes in small pieces. You should have about ½ cup. Finely chop enough basil leaves to make ½ cup. Set aside.

Combine flour, cheese, salt, pepper, baking powder, dehydrated tomato sauce and sugar until thoroughly blended. Slice butter into flour mixture, making sure each piece is coated with mixture. Using a pastry blender or wire whisk, press into the butter (as if you are mashing potatoes) until mixture has a sandy texture resembling fine crumbs. Add tomatoes and basil. Blend well.

In another bowl, beat egg and add half-and-half. Combine egg and flour mixtures just until ingredients are blended. Roll dough into a 12-inch log. Using your hands or a rolling pin, flatten log into a rectangle measuring 3 x 12 inches and ½- to ¾-inch thick. Make sure thickness is consistent throughout dough. Cut rectangle into 4 equal squares and cut each square in half diagonally, making 8 scones.

Evenly space scones on an ungreased cookie sheet. Bake for 15 to 20 minutes, or until bottoms are lightly browned. Serve warm.

INDEX